Celebrate Ash
North Carolina
Adult Coloring Book

By Lilt Kids Coloring Books

Copyright © 2016 by Lilt Kids Coloring Books

Sit back, relax, and enjoy this fun and funky coloring book that celebrates the beautiful and unique city of Asheville, NC. Nestled away in the Southern Appalachian Mountains, Asheville is known far and wide as a happy and creative place to live and visit. The area surrounding Asheville has many gorgeous views and scenic overlooks such as the ones featured in this book.

Also featured in this book are scenes from downtown Asheville which is popular for many different reasons including excellent quality musicians performing on the street corners, quirky characters, and so much more. Local beer is a very important part of Asheville culture and economy and it has been named Beer City, USA for three years in a row.

Asheville is truly a mix of hip and natural living and has a reputation for being a dog-friendly, kid-friendly, hippie-friendly and fun-loving place to be. So come celebrate all that is Asheville with this fabulous coloring book for adults

INDEX:

Helpful Tips for Coloring

~ Sometimes the colors appear differently on paper than what you would expect. Use the color test page to play with your colors beforehand.

~ If you are using colored pencils make sure to keep them sharp. This helps when coloring smaller areas or details on the page. Fine point sharpies also work great for smaller areas.

~ Speaking of sharpies, make sure you put a scrap piece of paper behind the page you are coloring to keep the markers from bleeding to the next page.

~ When using crayons or pencils start out light. You can always go back and darken later.

~ There are so many tools for coloring: markers, sharpies, crayons, pencils, pastels, and the list goes on. Experiment with what works best for you and your designs. Though it's not necessary, using higher quality coloring utensils makes a difference.

~ If you come to a design that seems overwhelming just pick a place to start and go from there. Once you begin your creativity will quickly take over!! If you get discouraged just take a break and come back to the page later.

~ Remember to practice. Like anything else, the more you do it the better you'll get. It'll become more and more relaxing each time.

~ DON'T FOLLOW THE RULES! It's up to you how you color your designs. Just let your creativity take the lead and HAVE FUN!

COLOR TEST PAGE

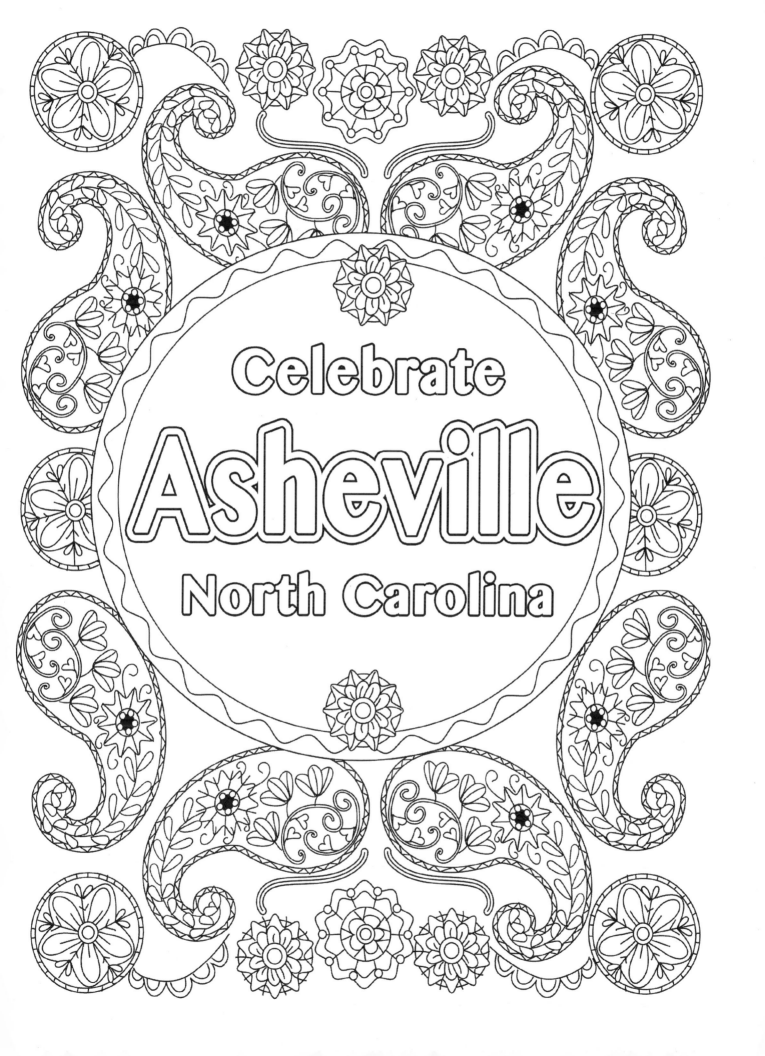

Celebrate

Asheville

North Carolina

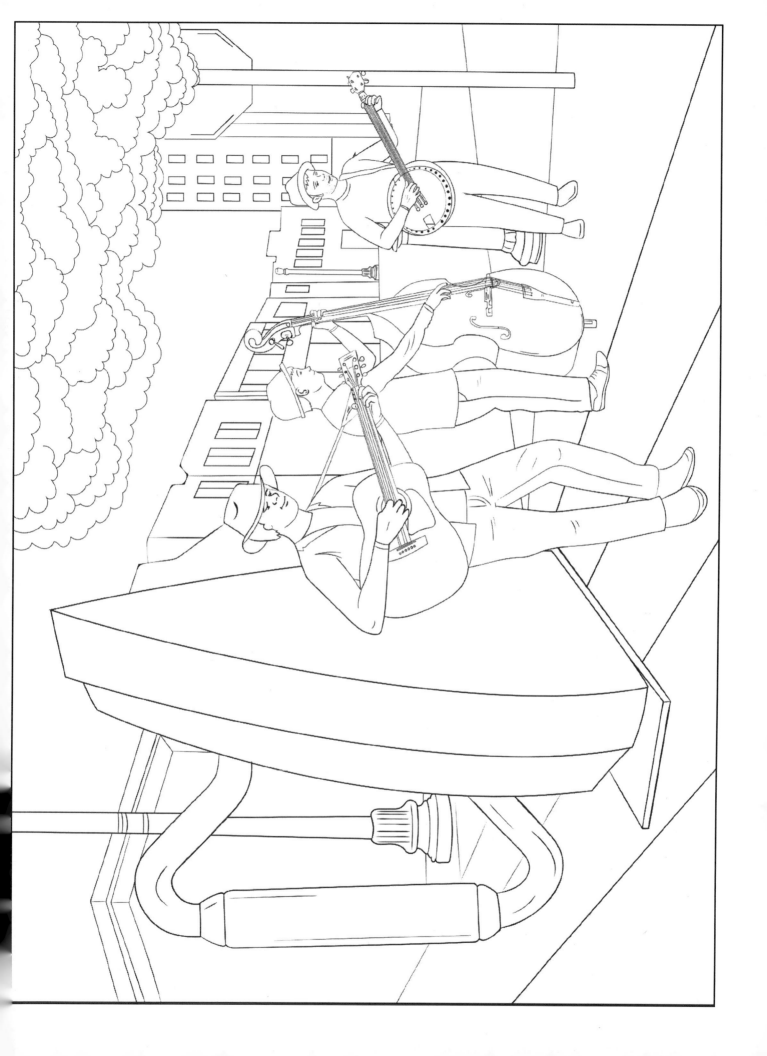

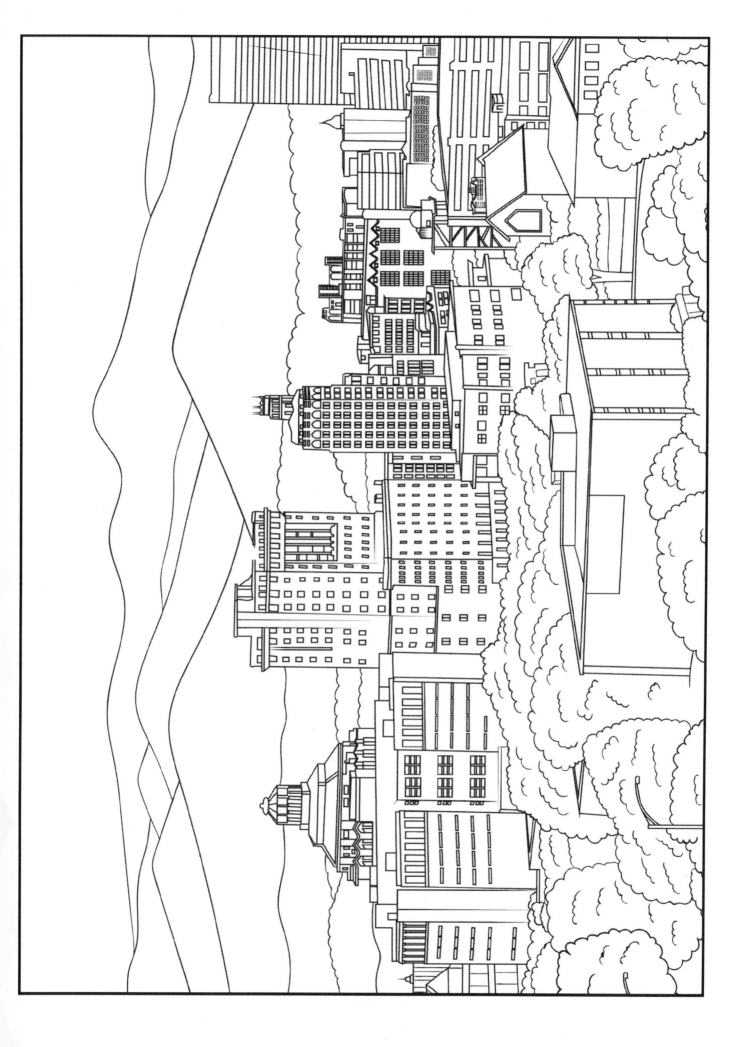

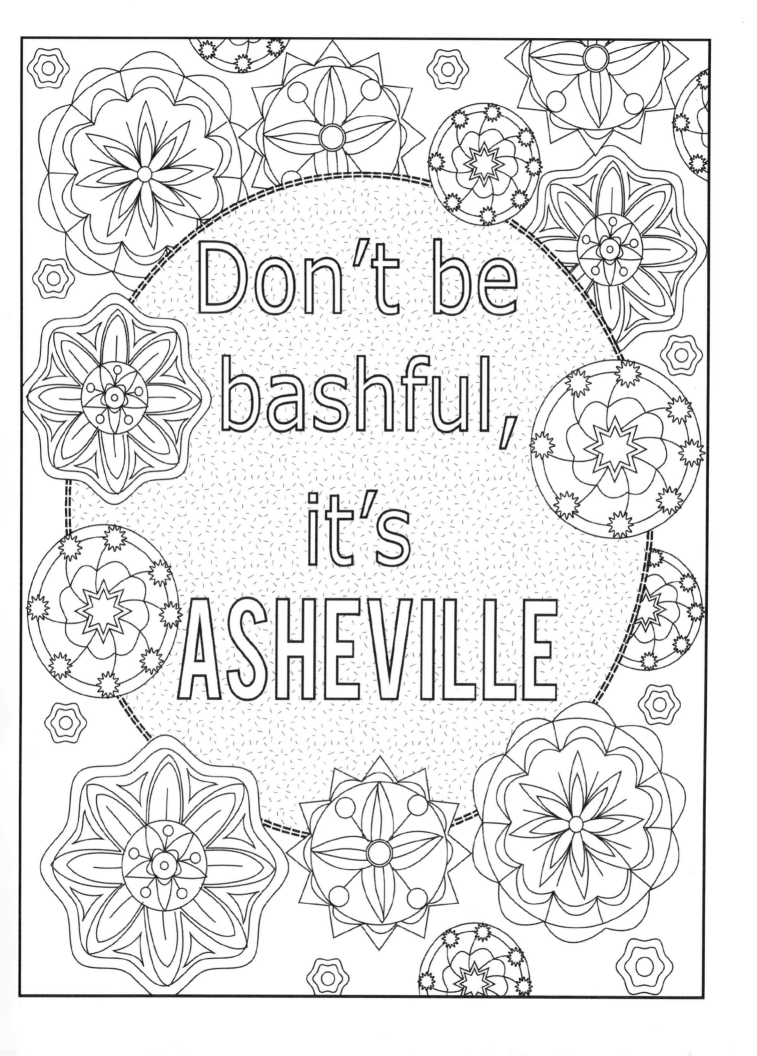

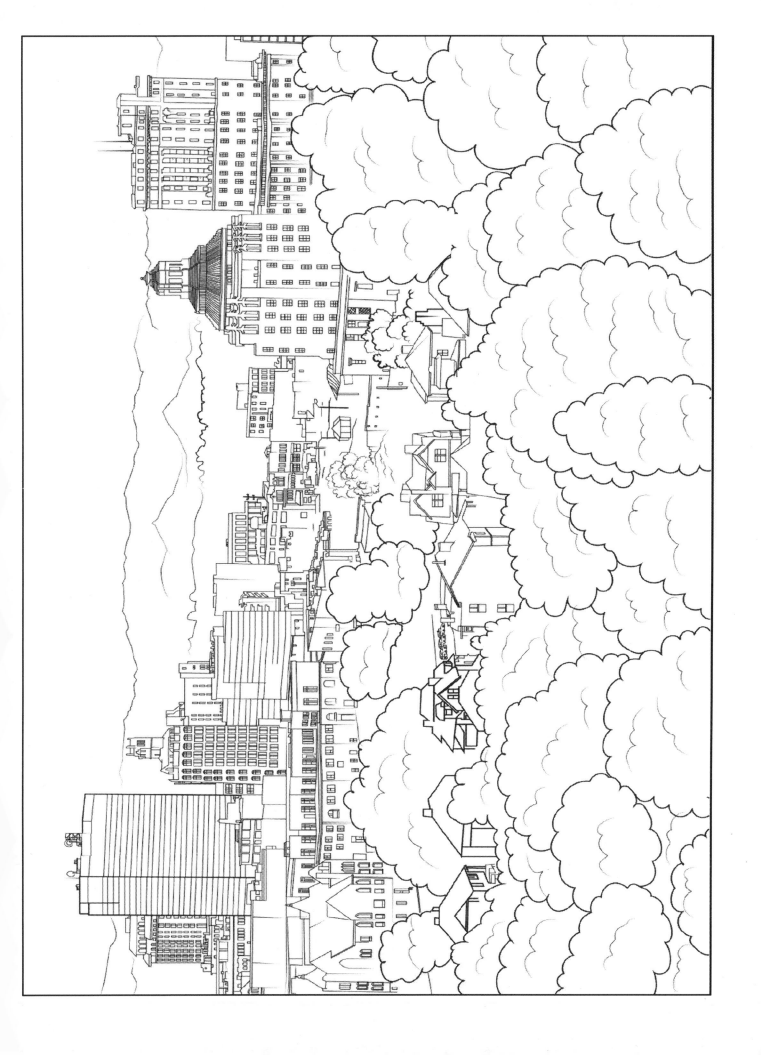

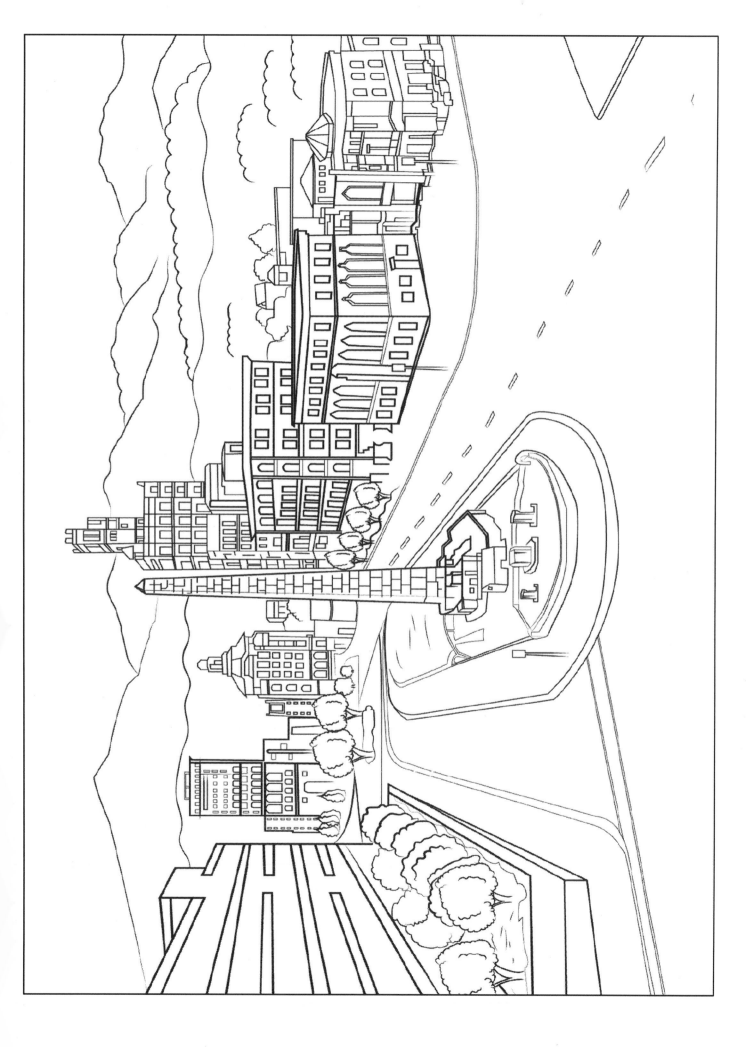

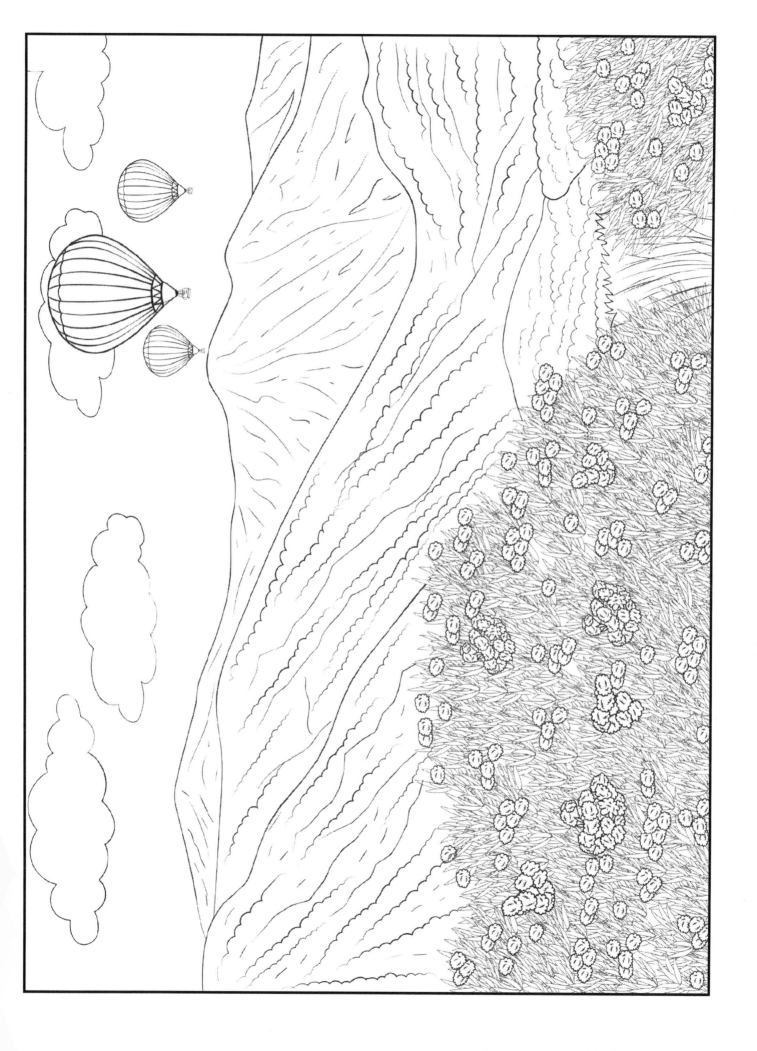

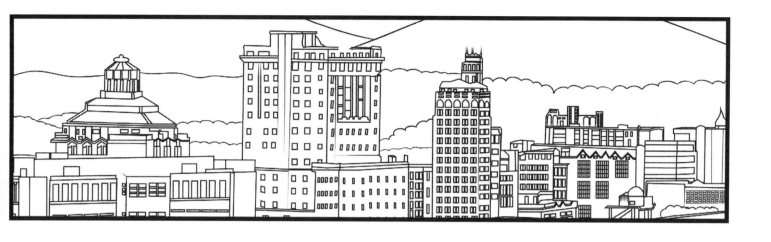

Made in the USA
Middletown, DE
19 July 2018